Interviewing Skills

About the series

Your Personal Trainer is a series of five books designed to help you learn, or develop, key business skills. Fun, flexible and involving (and written by experienced, real-life trainers), each title in the series acts as your very own 'personal fitness trainer', allowing you to focus on your own individual experience and identify priorities for action.

Assertiveness   1 904298 13 3
Stress Management 1 904298 17 6
Interviewing Skills   1 904298 14 1
Negotiating Skills   1 904298 15 X
Time Management   1 904298 16 8

Interviewing Skills

by Liz Edwards

First published in 2003 by
Spiro Press
17-19 Rochester Row
London SW1P 1LA
Telephone: +44 (0)870 400 1000

ISBN 1 904298 14 1

British Library Cataloguing-in-Publication Data.
A catalogue record for this book is available from the British Library.

Library of Congress Cataloging-in-Publication. Data on file.

Series devised by: Astrid French and Susannah Lear
Series Editor: Astrid French

Spiro Press USA
3 Front Street
Suite 331
PO Box 338
Rollinsford NH 03869
USA

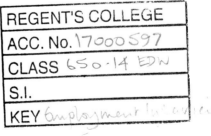

Typeset by: Wyvern 21 Ltd, Bristol
Printed in Great Britain by: Cromwell Press
Cover image by: Gettyimages
Cover design by: Cachet Creatives

Contents

Introduction

Welcome to *Interviewing Skills*, part of a series – **Your Personal Trainer** – which offers you an exciting new way to learn, or develop, key business skills. Fun, flexible and involving, each title in this series acts as your very own 'personal fitness trainer', allowing you to focus on your individual experience and identify priorities for action. Designed as a self-development workbook, each title creates an individual record of what you have achieved.

This book focuses on developing your *selection interviewing* skills – essential if you are involved in the process of 'hiring' people. It will help you to gain an insight into how to get the best from an interview and make a more informed decision about who you might, or might not, select for a particular role.

> *WATCH OUT FOR YOUR TRAINER*
> He will give you tips and alert you to potential areas of concern as you work your way through the book.

Everyone is capable of developing the skills of interviewing – once they understand what's involved and what to do when. Becoming 'fit' in interviewing terms may well be challenging. However, it will pay dividends in the long term by giving you the satisfaction of knowing you have prepared well and that the decisions you make are informed, professional and objective.

TRAINER'S WARNING

Seek professional advice on any legal issues around selection interviewing and the wider selection process before getting started.

What is interviewing?

There are many different types of interviews and interviewing techniques; this book focuses on selection interviewing, a key part of the selection process.

So, what do you gain, or lose, by developing your selection interviewing skills?

You gain:

✓ an appreciation of how the process works
✓ background knowledge about the skills involved and the confidence to go out and practise those skills
✓ the recognition that you are making informed decisions
✓ the knowledge that you are behaving professionally and keeping within the law.

You lose:

✗ some bad habits – if you are currently interviewing without any of the knowledge or background
✗ time to do other things; effective selection interviewing demands time and commitment.

And what do you gain, or lose, by not developing interviewing skills?

You gain:

✓ time to do other things
✓ the security of keeping within your current comfort zone.

You lose:

✗ the ability to participate in the recruitment process
✗ the knowledge that you are making informed decisions
✗ an understanding of the law
✗ possibly money, by making the wrong decision.

So, do you have more to gain by developing your interviewing skills than you have to lose? Would you give up some of the gains of not improving your skills for the security of knowing that you have become better and more effective at selecting people? If the answer is 'Yes', read on...

This is a book for anyone who wants to learn about selection interviewing and have some fun while doing so! Whether developing your interviewing skills from scratch, or brushing up on what you already know, enjoy your read, and enjoy the benefits of improved interviewing skills.

How to use this book

This book has been produced in a flexible format so you can maximize your individual potential for learning. You will have to put some work into it, but you should have some fun along the way.

The book is divided into four main parts:
Fitness Assessment
Fitness Profile
Work-out
Keeping Fit.

Fitness Assessment consists of 10 assessments. These assessments are grouped into three key skills areas or sections:

Preparation
Interviewing, and
Follow-up.

The assessments offer a range of questions, exercises and choices of behaviour to test your current skills fitness.

Try and be as honest as possible when completing this part so you have a realistic idea of your current 'fitness'. And remember, there are no wrong answers, only feedback!

Fitness Profile gives you the results of your Fitness Assessment. It helps you understand your responses and identify both personal strengths and weaknesses/areas for development.

Work-out offers a range of practical activities to improve your skills and help you to become a 'super-fit' interviewer.

Keeping Fit reminds you of the importance of practising your skills and allows you to develop a personal fitness plan.

You will get the most out of this book if you work through it systematically, checking up on your selection interviewing skills from 1-10. This will enable you to get a good overall view of your fitness.

However, you may choose to focus on a particular area of the skill (eg Preparation), working through the relevant section in Fitness Assessment, then moving on to subsequent sections in Fitness Profile and Work-out. These sections are clearly identified in the text, with directions to follow-up reading marked with an arrow *at the end of each section*.

Finally, if you want a quick review of key learning points, check out the summary checklists at the end of each section in Work-out.

Whichever way you choose to use this book, enjoy the experience!

Fitness Assessment

Fitness Assessment

Fitness Assessment has been designed to test your current skills fitness.

If you want an overall picture of your skills fitness (which is recommended), you need to work through all 10 assessments, then move on to subsequent parts – Fitness Profile, Work-out and Keeping Fit.

*If you don't want to work through all the assessments, or wish to focus your learning, you can concentrate on those sections which develop a particular aspect of the skill, and then only work through relevant subsequent sections. If you do decide to do this, however, make sure that you work through **all** the assessments within the individual sections.*

Assessments 1-3 *focus on* **Preparation**
Assessments 4-7 *on* **Interviewing**
Assessments 8-10 *on* **Follow-up.**

So, let's test your current skills fitness.

Preparation

Preparation is key to the success of selection interviewing.

Professional interviewers take time to take stock of the task, gather all the relevant information, organize the interviews and prepare themselves. And all of this before they even get to the interview!

The following three assessments will help you understand how well you prepare for interviews.

ASSESSMENT 1: YOUR APPROACH

How you approach any task, no matter how big or how small, will influence its eventual outcome.

Read through the following scenario; tick your most likely response.

TRAINER'S WARNING

Don't forget to answer these questions honestly; make sure you get a true picture of your fitness.

Your manager has asked you to attend an important meeting on his behalf. Would you:

A Clarify the objective and read up the documentation?   □ ✓

B Stay cool and deal with any questions as they come?   □

C Pester your manager about the meeting, and make – and remake – a list of actions?   □

D Assume documents will be there on the day – you don't have the time to read them before then anyway?   □

TRAINER'S TIP

Feel free to change the genders in any of the examples offered; you may find this helps you relate to the situations.

ASSESSMENT 2: GATHERING INFORMATION

Gathering information and relevant documents

is an important part of the selection interviewing process. How familiar are you with the documentation that is used in selection interviewing?

Look at the list of documents below. How much do you know about them? Circle either 1, 2, 3 or 4 as described in the following key.

KEY
1 = No knowledge **2** = A little knowledge
3 = A reasonable knowledge **4** = An excellent knowledge

Document

1	Job description	1	2	3	4
2	Person specification	1	2	3	4
3	Competency framework	1	2	3	4
4	Exit interview	1	2	3	4
5	Application form	1	2	3	4
6	Assessment form	1	2	3	4
7	Ethnic monitoring form	1	2	3	4
8	Curriculum vitae	1	2	3	4

Now add up your total score   SCORE

ASSESSMENT 3: ORGANIZING INTERVIEWS

Read through the following scenarios. Tick your most likely response.

1 You realize you should have allowed more time between the interviews you have arranged. What would you do?

   A Explain to the interviewers that they will have to work through without a break, or shorten some of the interviews. ☐

   B Reschedule the interviews and inform everyone. ☐

C Tell the candidates when they arrive that their
interviews will start later than planned.   ☐

2 You have to set up a room for interviews. Which of the
following layouts would you choose? (The rectangle
represents a desk, the two squares chairs.)

A

B

C

3 You have received copies of the documentation for
interviews you and your colleague will be conducting.
What would you do?
A Read through the documentation and identify
questions to ask each of the candidates.   ☐
B Hope your colleague will do the questioning and
volunteer yourself to make notes.   ☐

C   Discuss strategy with your colleague and agree
which areas each of you will cover and prepare
questions accordingly.   ☐

Ideally, you should work through all 10 assessments to get
an overall view of your interviewing fitness. If, however, you
wish to focus only on the preparation involved in the
interviewing process ➡ Preparation Fitness Profile p.25.

Interviewing

The interview is one of the most unreliable selection
methods. Too often an interviewer relies on that old chestnut
'gut feeling'. Interviewing needs more than gut feeling; it
needs effective preparation (as discussed already) and
appropriate communication skills used in a way that will get
the best from the candidates. So, what are those
communication skills?

Assessments 4-7 focus on the key communication skills you
will need to use when you undertake any interview.

TRAINER'S WARNING

*Make sure you
answer these
questions
honestly; make
sure you get a
true
picture of
your
fitness.*

ASSESSMENT 4: USING QUESTIONING
SKILLS

*Read through the following
questions/requests for
information and decide
whether they would be useful
in an interview. If you think
they would be useful put a
tick in the box; if not then put
a cross.*

TRAINER'S TIP

*Feel free to
change the
genders in any
of the examples
offered; you
may find this
helps
you
relate
to the
situations.*

1 'Tell me about your first job.' ☐
2 'You said you enjoyed decision-making. Give me
   an example of a good decision you have made.' ☐
3 'What would you do if you had to face an angry
   customer?' ☐
4 'Are you planning to have a family?' ☐
5 'What were the main objectives in your job; how
   did you achieve them and what was the result?' ☐
6 'Do you thrive on pressure?' ☐
7 'You were in that role six years. Is that correct?' ☐
8 'Don't you think communication is essential in
   managing staff?' ☐
9 'Your exam results are pretty poor – that must have
   annoyed you?' ☐
10 'You seem concerned about delegation. Why is that?'☐

ASSESSMENT 5: USING EFFECTIVE LISTENING SKILLS

Being able to listen effectively is a key skill; and no more so
than in an interview situation.

*How good are you at listening? Read through the statements
below and rate yourself according to the following key.*

KEY
1 = I never do this
2 = I sometimes do this
3 = I usually do this

1 I keep any distracting mannerism under
   control.   1   2   3
2 If I feel biased or prejudiced, I don't let it
   show.   1   2   3
3 Even if I am bored, I don't show it.   1   2   3

4 I maintain eye contact as appropriate. 1 2 3

5 I encourage with a nod, smile or a word
of agreement. 1 2 3

6 I focus on the other person not myself. 1 2 3

7 I find it easy to concentrate when
listening. 1 2 3

8 I control my emotions. 1 2 3

9 I don't interrupt. 1 2 3

10 I don't get impatient if the person isn't
getting the message across. 1 2 3

11 I judge what the person is saying rather
than the person. 1 2 3

12 I don't finish people's sentences for them. 1 2 3

13 I can ignore external distractions. 1 2 3

14 I try to reflect back information and
feelings. 1 2 3

15 I concentrate on the person not on what
I want to say next. 1 2 3

16 I summarize what has been said. 1 2 3

17 I don't draw instant conclusions. I wait
until the person has finished speaking. 1 2 3

18 I don't rush in whenever there is silence. 1 2 3

Now add up your total score   SCORE

ASSESSMENT 6: BODY LANGUAGE

TRAINER'S WARNING

People from different cultural backgrounds may use and interpret body language differently.

Your body talks! It is constantly sending out signals about how you think and feel about yourself, situations and other people – body language. This body language is then picked up and interpreted by those around you. You need to be aware of your body language, and other people's. Again, this is no truer than in an interview situation.

In face-to-face communication, body language accounts for some 55% of someone's impression of you, voice 38%, content only 7%.

How good are you at interpreting body language signals? Read through the following examples of body language and suggest what each one might mean (eg surprise, interest, tension, nervousness, lying). (One has been done to illustrate.)

Head nodding   ***Agreement disagreement***

A Raised eyebrows ....
....
B Making eye contact ....
....
C Avoiding eye contact ....
....
D Smiling mouth ....
....
E Fingering the collar ....
....
F Hunched shoulders ....
....
G Hands over mouth..
....
H Arms crossed ....
....
I Hands wringing, clenched ....
....
J Legs tight against body ....
....
K Leaning forwards ....
....
L Sudden movement forwards ....
....
M Sudden movement backwards ....

ASSESSMENT 7: BUILDING A RAPPORT

People can be nervous at interviews – interviewers as well as candidates! Building a rapport can help quieten nerves, and encourage honest, calm communication.

Read through the scenarios below and decide whether or not the interviewers are behaving in a 'helping' or 'hindering' manner.

Put a tick in the box if 'helping', a cross if 'hindering'.

1 Ann met the candidates at the door, shook hands, and greeted them with 'Hello there, thank you for coming. My name is Ann Brown.' ☐

2 Interview candidate Simon seemed distressed at being unable to answer a couple of questions. Janet responded quickly, 'Well, never mind, they're not that important.' ☐

3 Personnel manager Phil could see Chandu was very nervous, so he spent ten minutes talking about his own love – cricket – as Chandu had listed it as one of his hobbies. ☐

4 Jane was a school leaver and very apprehensive at the interview. The personnel officer, Lesley, knew her voice could be intimidating so she spoke quietly and slowly. ☐

5 Neisha had been delayed by a large pile-up on the motorway so Rory offered her some refreshments when she arrived for interview. ☐

6 Chris liked to conduct interviews informally in the low, soft chairs away from his desk. ☐

7 Mary's desk was very imposing so she used a smaller, round table for conducting interviews. ☐

8 Scott liked to give the candidates a lower chair than his – that way he could show who was in charge.   ☐

9 After the introductions, Terry said, 'I would like to talk to you about your current role and how your experience might meet our needs, John. Is that OK?'   ☐

10 Emer was having difficulty clarifying her answers, so Fran encouraged her, on a number of occasions, by finishing her sentences.   ☐

11 Robbie explained to each candidate that he would be taking notes as he wanted to be sure he had an accurate record of the event.   ☐

12 Jenny had an excellent academic background and was being interviewed by Mel whose qualifications came from the 'University of Life'. He used his technical knowledge and business jargon to impress her.   ☐

13 Liz's answers were long and rambling and the interview was taking longer than Pridath intended. He started looking at his watch, hoping this would 'stem the flow'.   ☐

14 The Chair of the panel introduced each of the members to the candidates, explaining what their roles would be during the interview.   ☐

Ideally, you should work through all 10 assessments to get an overall view of your skills fitness. If, however, you wish to focus on the skills involved in carrying out the interview itself ➡ Interviewing Fitness Profile p.31.

Follow-up

This third section looks at the last stage in the interview process – evaluating the candidates, informing them of the outcome and reviewing the process.

ASSESSMENT 8: EVALUATING

Evaluating candidates can seem a daunting task. To succeed, you need to be clear about the nature of the job and then judge people's suitability in terms of their skills, experience and personal attributes. It can be helpful to draw up a list of 'essential' and 'desirable' criteria.

Read through the following scenarios and decide which of the candidates you would choose in each case.

1   Candidates for the Sales and Marketing Director's PA vacancy were assessed against a range of essential and desirable criteria.

	Candidate		
	A	B	C
Essential criteria			
• Microsoft Office suite	✓	✓	✓
• Advanced PowerPoint	✓	✓	✗
• Excellent communication skills	✗	✓	✓
• Teamworker	✓	✓	✓
• Able to work in a pressurized environment	✓	✓	?
• Sales and marketing background	✓	✓	✗

Desirable criteria

- Experience at a senior secretarial level   ✓ ✗ ✓
- Shorthand   ✗ ✓ ✓
- Experience of organizing conferences   ✓ ✗ ✓
- Knowledge of Spanish   ✓ ✗ ✗
- Desktop publishing experience   ✓ ✗ ✓

Your choice as the 'best' candidate   ☐

> **TRAINER'S TIP**
>
> *The job cannot be done without the essential criteria. Desirable criteria are a bonus and may help the potential employee be effective more quickly.*

2   A shortlist of candidates had been interviewed a second time for a Distribution Office Team Leader. The criteria have been weighted according to their importance to the role.

^{1} = Most important
^{7} = Least important

The candidates were given marks out of 10; their scores are outlined below.

		Candidate A	B	C
Appearance	6	8	5	8
Qualifications	7	9	5	7
Experience	2	4	7	5
Knowledge	5	9	7	7
Skills/Abilities	1	7	7	6
Test scores	3	7	9	8
Personal qualities	4	6	9	8
Total				

Your choice as the 'best' candidate   ☐

3 The three candidates for the position of Accounts Clerk were interviewed by both the line manager and a personnel officer. They assessed them using the gradings below.

4 = Exceeds requirements of job
3 = Meets requirements of job
2 = Falls slightly below requirements of job
1 = Falls well short of the requirements of the job

	Candidate		
	A	B	C
Line manager			
Computer inputting skills (test)	4	3	3
Knowledge	4	4	2
Experience	3	4	1
Numeracy (test)	3	3	3
Teamworking	3	4	4
Organizational skills	2	3	3
Personal attributes	3	3	4
Total			
Personnel officer			
Computer inputting skills (test)	4	3	3
Knowledge	3	4	3
Experience	4	4	3
Numeracy (test)	3	3	3
Teamworking	2	3	4
Organizational skills	3	3	4
Personal attributes	3	3	4
Total			
Overall total			

Your choice as the 'best' candidate ☐

ASSESSMENT 9: INFORMING CANDIDATES

Read through the following scenarios and tick the most appropriate option.

1 The line manager has made his decision and passed the information on to you for finalizing. Would you:
   A Reject all the unsucessful candidates immediately in writing? ☐
   B Wait until the selected candidate has accepted before rejecting all the others? ☐
   C Keep two reserves and reject all the others immediately? ☐

2 You have been asked to reject the unsuccessful candidates. Would you:
   A Send individual letters? ☐
   B Send standard rejection letters? ☐
   C Telephone each of them? ☐

3 You have rejected the unsuccessful candidates. One of them telephones for feedback. Would you:
   A Refuse? ☐
   B Give vague, general feedback? ☐
   C Give specific feedback? ☐

4 The short-listed candidates were of a very high standard but unfortunately there was only one vacancy. As a big organization, you are constantly recruiting. Would you:
   A Keep their details on file for a few months? ☐
   B Destroy all their details? ☐
   C Pass their details on to colleagues who might be interested in them? ☐

ASSESSMENT 10: REVIEWING THE PROCESS

To improve your interviewing skills you need to review your performance – and the process – regularly.

What should be included in a review? Read through the list below and decide which items should be included. Put a tick in the box if you think they should be included, a cross if not.

A   An assessment of your own performance.   ☐

B   Feedback on your performance from any other interviewers involved.   ☐

C   Revisit your initial assessment and compare your judgement of the new recruit then with how you view him/her now.   ☐

D   Compare the number of applications against previous selection exercises.   ☐

E   Feedback from the line manager on how the new recruit is settling in and performing in the role.   ☐

F   Feedback from the new recruit.   ☐

G   Feedback on the new recruit from others such as peers and customers.   ☐

H   Feedback from the line manager on the handling of the process.   ☐

I   Review the selection process overall.   ☐

J   Monitor the process for gender, ethnic group and/or disability discrimination.   ☐

K   Review the cost of the process against other selection efforts.   ☐

L   Compare the length of the process against other selection exercises.   ☐

M   Assess the cost of the process against its perceived benefits.   ☐

Ideally, you will now have completed all 10 assessments and tested your overall skills fitness. If so ➡ Fitness Profile p.21.

If you have chosen to focus on your follow-up skills ➡ Follow-up Fitness Profile p.41.

Fitness Profile

Well done, you've gone through the Fitness Assessment – now you can find out the results!

Fitness Profile allows you to evaluate your current skills fitness – strengths, weaknesses and priorities for action. It builds up into a fitness profile unique to you.

Fitness profiles 1-3 relate directly to assessments 1-3. Similarly, profiles 4-7 and 8-10 relate directly to assessments 4-7 and 8-10.

Preparation

The following three profiles will help you assess how well you prepare for interviews.

PROFILE 1: YOUR APPROACH

Look back to assessment 1 (p.5); remind yourself of the scenario and make a note of the option (A-D) you ticked here   ☐

For this question the most appropriate answer is **A** (clarify the objective and read up the documentation). If you selected this answer, you have a healthy attitude to preparation

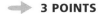 **3 POINTS**

If you selected **B** (stay cool and deal with any questions as they come), you could be too casual in your approach to preparation. Being laid back seems cool, but without some contingency built in you could end up floored

1 POINT

If you opted for **C** (pester your manager about the meeting; make and remake a list of actions), you could over-prepare, which could have a detrimental effect. You could end up not getting anything right because you spend more time worrying, or worrying others!   **2 POINTS**

If you selected **D** (assume documents will be there on the day), you may be having difficulty planning your time. If you don't make time, you may 'miss the boat' altogether

1 POINT

SCORE

For assessment 1, the higher you score the better your approach to tasks and that vital first stage – preparation. You have a better chance of getting the job done successfully.
The **maximum** score is **3**.
The **minimum** score is **1**.

PROFILE 2: GATHERING INFORMATION

Look back to assessment 2 (p.5); remind yourself of the question and your responses. Now make a note of your score for this question here   SCORE

For assessment 2 the higher you score the more comfortable you are with the documentation used in selection interviewing.
The **maximum** score is **32**.
The **minimum** score is **8**.

PROFILE 3: ORGANIZING INTERVIEWS

Look back to p.6 in Fitness Assessment to remind yourself of the scenarios in assessment 3, and how you responded. Now make a note of the options (A-C) you ticked below.

	A	B	C
Question 1	☐	☐	☐
Question 2	☐	☐	☐
Question 3	☐	☐	☐

QUESTION 1
You realize you should have allowed more time between the interviews you have arranged. What would you do?

For question 1 the preferred response is **B**, reschedule the interviews and inform everyone. Although this may be a pain, it is fairer all round **3 POINTS**

If you chose **A** (explain to the interviewers that they will have to work through without a break, or shorten some of the interviews) **1 POINT**

Interviewers must have some 'breathing space' to gather their thoughts, make notes and have a 'comfort break'. Also, if each candidate is to be treated fairly, they must be allocated a similar amount of time to 'sell' themselves.

If you chose **C** (tell candidates when they arrive that their interviews will start later than planned) **1 POINT**

This is simply not courteous. You should not expect candidates to wait when they have been given a specific appointment time. Remember, they will be assessing your organization as well! Delaying them will not give a good impression of you.

SCORE

QUESTION 2

You have to set up a room for interviews. Which of the following layouts would you choose?

A

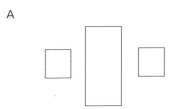

An interview should be a reasonably stress-free, two-way dialogue and will be more successful if you and the candidate are not separated by a desk ➡ **1 POINT**

B

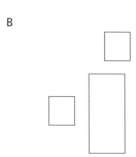

This is probably the best option – it gives both interviewer and candidate somewhere to put their papers. However, if a round table is available this would be better still. Make sure the seats are comfortable ➡ **3 POINTS**

C

This is an option also, but you would have to be careful to make sure the chairs are sufficiently far apart to avoid invading a candidate's personal space ➡ **1 POINT**

SCORE

QUESTION 3

You have received copies of the documentation for interviews you and your colleague will be conducting. What would you do?

For question 3 the preferred response is **C** – discuss strategy with your colleague and agree which areas each of you will cover and prepare questions accordingly

 **3 POINTS**

This is the best choice. It is essential that you decide your strategy in advance and identify the specific areas each of you is going to cover in the interview.

If you chose **A** – read through the documentation and identify questions to ask each of the candidates

 **1 POINT**

You and your colleague could end up covering the same ground. This would be both a time-waster and an irritant for the candidates. It could indicate also that you, and the organization, is unprofessional

If you chose **B** – hope your colleague will do the questioning and volunteer yourself to make notes

 1 POINT

An interview with more than one person can be intimidating enough for candidates without one of them being silent throughout. Anyway, what if your colleague has had the same idea?

SCORE

Now add up your scores

TOTAL ASSESSMENT 3 SCORE

For assessment 3, the higher you score the better you organize interviews.
The **maximum** score is **9**.
The **minimum** score is **3**.

TRAINER'S WARNING

Where more than one interviewer is involved, make sure you stick to your agreed focus areas.

So, how healthy are your preparation skills? Look back to p.25 for your score for assessment 1 and write it down here ☐
Now your assessment 2 score ☐
Now your assessment 3 score ☐

Add these individual scores together to make your **total preparation score:**

TOTAL PREPARATION SCORE

The higher your total score the better your approach to, and skills of, preparation.
The **maximum** score is **44**.
The **minimum** score is **12**.

General areas of exploration at interview include:
- *whether they can do the job (ie skills and experience)*
- *if they will do the job (ie commitment, enthusiasm and motivation)*
- *if they will fit in (ie values, 'personality')*
- *why they are applying and what interests them about the job.*

over 36

Congratulations, you have a healthy approach to preparation, and good skills. There is always room for improvement, however!

28-35

You are getting there. In general, you have a good grasp of the preparation stage but there are one or two weaker areas. With a good work-out you should be able to improve.

20-27 You have a grasp of the importance of the preparation stage in the interviewing process, and some skills. However, there are a number of weaknesses and you need to make improvements.

 12-19 You seem to be unaware of the importance of preparing for interviews and are unfit. You need to work-out.

Ideally, you should work through all 10 assessments, profiles and work-outs to improve your overall fitness. If you wish to focus on improving your preparation ➡ Preparation work-out p.59. Before doing this, however, it is wise to do some quick mental preparation ➡ Warm-up p.53.

Interviewing

Assessments 4-7 focused on your communication skills – key to effective interviewing. Let's see how you got on.

PROFILE 4: USING QUESTIONING SKILLS

Go back to p.8 to remind yourself of assessment 4. Make a note of your responses (✓/✗) below.

1	☐	**6**	☐
2	☐	**7**	☐
3	☐	**8**	☐
4	☐	**9**	☐
5	☐	**10**	☐

Give yourself 2 POINTS for each correct answer.

TRAINER'S TIP

Use 'closed' questions if you want a specific 'Yes' or 'No' answer and 'open' questions if you want to encourage the candidate to give information.

Open questions usually begin with 'Who?', 'When?', 'What?', 'Where?', 'How?', 'Why?', 'Tell me...'

1 'Tell me about your first job.'   ✓

This is an open question that encourages the
candidate to talk.

2 'You said you enjoyed decision-making. Give me an
example of a good decision you have made.'   ✓

This is another open question, but a 'probing' one
this time: used to get further information.

3 'What would you do if you had to face an angry
customer?'   ✗

This is a hypothetical question and candidates are
likely to give answers that put them in the best
possible light, such as 'I would be calm, efficient and
empathetic.'

4 'Are you planning to have a family?'   ✗

This is a personal, discriminatory question and should
not be asked.

5 'What were the main objectives in your job; how did
you achieve them and what was the result?'   ✗

A multiple question – three questions in one! A
skilled candidate will just answer the question that
suits them.

6 'Do you thrive on pressure?'   ✗

A closed, cliché question. An experienced candidate
will have a pat answer for this, such as 'Yes – I go

looking for it!' A better way to get the information would be: 'This job will involve working at a fast pace. Give me an example of when you had to work under extreme pressure.'

7 'You were in that role six years. Is that correct?'   ✓

A closed question used to check facts and appropriate in this instance.

8 'Don't you think communication is essential in managing staff?'   ✗

This is a leading question. Leading questions are really statements by the interviewer and all they do is force candidates into answers they think you want.

9 'Your exam results are pretty poor – that must have annoyed you?'   ✗

A critical question that is making an assumption and could make a candidate defensive. If the results are relevant, a better question would be: 'Were you disappointed in your results?'

10 'You seem concerned about delegation. Why is that?' ✓

This is a reflective question which helps a candidate to think about something they have said and helps to clarify their attitudes, values and feelings.

Now add up your scores

TOTAL ASSESSMENT 4 SCORE

TRAINER'S WARNING

There are discrimination laws that dictate what you can and cannot ask in interview. These laws differ from country to country. Make sure you know what applies *before carrying out an interview.*

For assessment 4, the higher you score the more likely you are to be aware of the types of questions that are appropriate and helpful for interviews and those that are not.

The **maximum** score is **20**.
The **minimum** score is **0**.

PROFILE 5: USING EFFECTIVE LISTENING SKILLS

Look back to assessment 5 (p.9); remind yourself of the statements and your responses. Make a note of your score here ☐

For assessment 5, the higher you score the better you are at listening.

The **maximum** score is **54**.
The **minimum** score is **18**.

PROFILE 6: BODY LANGUAGE

Look back at assessment 6 (p.10); remind yourself of the examples of body language, and what you thought they meant. Now see how your suggestions compare with the following.

Give yourself 5 POINTS for a 'spot on' answer, 2 POINTS if you were in the right area and 0 POINTS if you were 'off beam' or left a blank.

A Raised eyebrows **surprise, shock**   ☐
B Making eye contact **interest**   ☐
C Avoiding eye contact **embarrassment, lying**   ☐
D Smiling mouth **friendliness, genuine**   ☐
E Fingering the collar **possibly not telling the
   truth**   ☐
F Hunched shoulders **tension**   ☐
G Hands over mouth **may not be telling the truth**   ☐
H Arms crossed **defensiveness, cold, comfortable**   ☐
I Hands wringing, clenched **nervousness**   ☐
J Legs tight against body **nervousness**   ☐
K Leaning forwards **interest, listening**   ☐
L Sudden movement forwards **aggression**   ☐
M Sudden movement backwards **surprise/shock**   ☐

Now add your scores together

TOTAL ASSESSMENT 6 SCORE

TRAINER'S WARNING

*Beware of making
assumptions! Body*

*language
can be
open to
different
interpretations.*

For assessment 6, the higher you score the better you appear to be at deciphering other people's body language.
The **maximum** score is **65**.
The **minimum** score is **0**.

PROFILE 7: BUILDING A RAPPORT

Look back to assessment 7 (p.11) and remind yourself of the scenarios; then make a note of your responses (✓/✗) below.

1	☐	**8**	☐
2	☐	**9**	☐
3	☐	**10**	☐
4	☐	**11**	☐
5	☐	**12**	☐
6	☐	**13**	☐
7	☐	**14**	☐

Give yourself 3 POINTS for each correct answer.

1 Ann met the candidates at the door, shook hands, and greeted them with 'Hello there, thank you for coming. My name is Ann Brown.'   ✓
Remember, the interview is not just about the candidate, it's also about you and the impression you give.   ☐

2 Interview candidate Simon seemed distressed at being unable to answer a couple of questions. Janet responded quickly, 'Well, never mind, they're not that important.'   ✗
This is not only unprofessional but rude. If the questions are not important, why ask them?   ☐

3 Personnel manager Phil could see Chandu was very nervous, so he spent ten minutes talking about his own love – cricket – as Chandu had listed it as one of his hobbies.   ✗
Being calm and allowing the candidate time to think and answer is the way to help them relax and build that all-important rapport.   ☐

4 Jane was a school leaver and very apprehensive at the interview. The personnel officer, Lesley, knew her voice could be intimidating so she spoke quietly and slowly.   ✗
This could be patronizing. You should try not to rush things, and give nervous candidates time to think.   ☐

5 Neisha had been delayed by a large pile-up on the motorway so Rory offered her some refreshments when she arrived for interview.   ✓
It is up to you whether or not to offer refreshments. However, it is important to have refreshments available for someone who has had a long journey.   ☐

6 Chris liked to conduct interviews informally in the low, soft chairs away from his desk.   ✗
Low, soft chairs put the candidate at a disadvantage and do not help build a rapport.   ☐

7 Mary's desk was very imposing so she used a smaller, round table for conducting interviews.   ✓
If the desk is imposing, try to find an alternative or place yourself and the candidate at angles.   ☐

8 Scott liked to give the candidates a lower chair than his – that way he could show who was in charge.   ✗
This is not behaviour conducive to building a rapport. Make sure you have chairs of equal height for you and the candidates.   ☐

9 After the introductions, Terry said, 'I would like to talk to you about your current role and how your experience might meet our needs, John. Is that OK?', ✓
This is how you should try to start your interviews.   ☐

10 Emer was having difficulty clarifying her answers, so

Fran encouraged her, on a number of occasions, by finishing her sentences. ✗

Don't be tempted to finish candidates' sentences. It is rude, intimidating and will not make the candidate feel any better. ☐

TRAINER'S WARNING

Beware of doodling or writing anything contentious that could be challenged later – check out the legal issues!

11 Robbie explained to each candidate that he would be taking notes as he wanted to be sure he had an accurate record of the event. ✓

Jot down key points only and maintain eye contact as much as possible. Make a note specifically if candidates are highlighting information they think is important. ☐

12 Jenny had an excellent academic background and was being interviewed by Mel whose qualifications came from the 'University of Life'. He used his technical knowledge and business jargon to impress her. ✗

Don't be tempted to use technical language or jargon; they are likely to hinder you – and your organization. ☐

13 Liz's answers were long and rambling and the interview was taking longer than Pridath intended. He started looking at his watch, hoping this would 'stem the flow'. ✗

Summarize to bring a particular discussion to a close and use open questions to get short, specific answers. ☐

14 The Chair of the panel introduced each of the members to the candidates, explaining what their roles would be during the interview ✓

It is important that the Chair should attempt to put candidates at their ease by going through these preliminaries. It is also courteous to make introductions – something that can be overlooked in interviewing. ☐

Strategy is essential for panel interviews. Each interviewer must know what areas they are covering otherwise there may be gaps or overlaps. Gaps or overlaps are not only unprofessional but they make you vulnerable to exploitation.

Now add up your scores

TOTAL ASSESSMENT 7 SCORE

For assessment 7 the higher you score the better you are at building rapport.
The **maximum** score is **42**.
The **minimum** score is **0**.

So, how fit are your interviewing skills?

Look back to p.33 for your score for assessment 4 and write it here ☐
Now your assessment 5 score ☐
Now your assessment 6 score ☐
Now your assessment 7 score ☐

Add these individual scores together to make your **total interviewing score:**

TOTAL INTERVIEWING SCORE

The higher your total score the more effective you are in conducting interviews.
The **maximum** score is **181**.
The **minimum** score is **18**.

over 141 Well done, you already have a healthy level of the skills, knowledge and behaviour needed to be an effective interviewer. There is always room for a tone-up, however!

100-140 You have a reasonable grasp of some aspects of interviewing and are fairly skills fit. However, interviewing is a costly business and deals with that precious commodity – people; it needs to be approached professionally. This means being fully conversant with all aspects of interviewing. A structured work-out should improve your performance.

59-99 You seem to be aware of some of the skills and behaviour necessary for interviewing. However, there is a way to go – a good work-out is called for!

18-58 As yet, you don't have the skills necessary to be an effective interviewer. You need to develop and practise the skills which, in turn, will lead to the appropriate professional behaviour.

Ideally, you should work through all 10 assessments, profiles and work-outs to improve your overall fitness. If, however, you wish to focus on improving your skills of interviewing ➡ Interviewing work-out p.69. Before doing this it is a good idea to do some quick mental preparation ➡ Warm-up p.53.

Follow-up

You may think that once you have completed the interviews your job is over, but think again! You have to evaluate the candidates, inform them of your decision and review the process and your efforts. The following three profiles will help you assess how fit you are at performing these important tasks.

PROFILE 8: EVALUATING

Look back to assessment 8 (p.14); remind yourself of the scenarios and how you responded (which candidate you selected). Circle your responses (A-C) below.

Look back to assessment 8 (p.14)

TRAINER'S WARNING

Don't be lured by 'desirable' criteria if someone doesn't meet the essentials.

1 Sales and Marketing Director's PA   **A B C**
2 Distribution Office Team Leader   **A B C**
3 Accounts Clerk   **A B C**

How did you do?

QUESTION 1
PA vacancy
Candidate **A** doesn't have all the essential criteria for the job. If her communication skills don't meet the standard, she should be rejected
➡ **1 POINT**

The best candidate is **B** as she meets all the essential criteria despite only meeting one of the desirable criteria   ➡ **3 POINTS**

Candidate **C** only meets three of the essential criteria and should be rejected
➡ **0 POINTS**

TRAINER'S TIP

Communication skills can be assessed via the interview discussion, comprehension tests and verbal reasoning.

SCORE

QUESTION 2
Distribution Office Team Leader

These were the best candidates from a larger group seen previously so it was likely scores would be close. At this stage, it is important to check how each one does against the more important criteria. When you do this, you'll see that you should have selected Candidate **B**. Although he had the lowest total score, the four most important criteria added up to more than those of the other two candidates, as shown below.

If you selected **B** ➡ **3 POINTS**
If you selected **A** ➡ **0 POINTS**
If you selected **C** ➡ **1 POINT**

SCORE

Candidate		A	B	C
Total overall scores		50	49	49
Skills/Abilities	1	7	7	6
Experience	2	4	7	5
Test scores	3	7	9	8
Personal qualities	4	6	9	8
Totals for the four most important criteria		**24**	**32**	**27**

TRAINER'S WARNING

When using a rating scale, be careful about adding all the scores together to get the 'best' candidate. For example, an outstanding rating on qualifications may be less relevant to job performance than ability.

QUESTION 3
Accounts Clerk vacancy

Check out the interviewers' scores opposite. If the interviewers' scores had been taken individually, the line manager's choice would have been Candidate B and the personnel officer's Candidate C. However, when the scores are totalled, Candidate **B** comes out as the best choice.

Candidate	A	B	C
Total – line manager	22	24	20
Total – personnel officer	22	23	24
Overall totals	**44**	**47**	**44**

If you selected A ➡ **0 POINTS** SCORE ☐
If you selected B ➡ **3 POINTS** SCORE ☐
If you selected C ➡ **1 POINT** SCORE ☐

SCORE

Now add up your scores

TOTAL ASSESSMENT 8 SCORE

For assessment 8 the higher you score the better your evaluating skills. The maximum score is **9**. The minimum score is **0**.

PROFILE 9: INFORMING CANDIDATES

It is important that candidates are informed about the outcome of an interview as quickly as possible.

QUESTION 1

The line manager has made his decision and passed the information to you for finalizing. What would you do?

A Reject all the unsuccessful candidates immediately in writing.
   If you opt for this course of action, and your first choice candidate doesn't accept the job, you are left without any reserve ➡ **1 POINT**

B Wait until the selected candidate has accepted before rejecting all the other candidates.
   You shouldn't keep all the unsuccessful candidates

waiting until your preferred candidate has accepted –
this could be some time! ➡ **3 POINTS**

C Keep two reserves and reject all the others
immediately.
This is the best answer in the circumstances. One of the
'reserves' may well be acceptable should your first
choice refuse, but they are less likely to accept if they
know they are 'second best' ➡ **5 POINTS**

SCORE

QUESTION 2

You have been asked to reject the unsuccessful candidates.
What would you do?

A Send individual letters.
This is the preferred answer. The candidates have given
their time for the interview – you should show courtesy
by writing to them individually and being as positive as
possible ➡ **5 POINTS**

B Send a standard rejection letter.
A standard rejection letter does nothing for the
corporate image or you, nor does it take account of the
feelings of the candidate ➡ **1 POINT**

C Telephone each of them.
Candidates deserve more than a phone call – unless
agreed in advance. A call could be followed up with a
letter. If you do reject candidates by phone, be
prepared to give feedback ➡ **3 POINTS**

SCORE

QUESTION 3

You have rejected the unsuccessful candidates. One of them
telephones for feedback; how would you respond?

A Refuse.
More and more candidates want feedback
so, where possible, you should be
prepared to give this   **1 POINT**

B Give vague, general feedback.
You should be prepared to discuss
candidates' performance in a constructive,
positive way   **1 POINT**

C Give specific feedback   **5 POINTS**

SCORE

QUESTION 4

The short-listed candidates were of a very high standard but
unfortunately there was only one vacancy. As a big
organization, you are constantly recruiting. What would you
do?

A Keep their details on file for a few months.
Today's reject may be tomorrow's employee – this is a
good idea    **5 POINTS**

B Destroy all their details.
What a waste! You could have potential employees at
your fingertips    **1 POINT**

C Pass their details on to colleagues who might be
interested in them.
Candidates who are unsuitable for one vacancy may
well be appropriate for something else
         **5 POINTS**

SCORE

TOTAL ASSESSMENT 9 SCORE

For assessment 9, the higher you score the more you recognize the importance of advising candidates of the outcome of interviews quickly and positively.
The **maximum** score is **20**. The **minimum** score is **4**.

PROFILE 10: REVIEWING THE PROCESS

Look back to assessment 10 on p.18; remind yourself of the items (A-M) listed and whether you thought they should be included in a review or not. Make a note of your responses (✓/✗) below.

A	☐	H	☐
B	☐	I	☐
C	☐	J	☐
D	☐	K	☐
E	☐	L	☐
F	☐	M	☐
G	☐		

Give yourself 5 POINTS for each correct answer.

A   An assessment of your own performance   ✓
    Identify personal performance aims at the outset; any review should relate to the achievement of these aims. Go through each aspect of your role in the process and identify anything you might do differently next time.

SCORE

B   Feedback on your performance from any other interviewers involved   ✓
    Ask for specific, constructive feedback on how you performed at each stage in the process. Develop a set of questions for the purpose. The feedback should focus on your aims.

SCORE

C   Revisit your initial assessment and compare your
    judgement of the new recruit then with how you view
    him/her now   ✓
    If you get to know the new recruits you may find it
    worthwhile to review your interview reactions against
    your current thoughts. Ensure you are clear about your
    objective if you do re-assess.

    SCORE

D   Compare the number of applications against previous
    selection exercises   ✗
    Unless you are comparing like with like you won't get
    meaningful data.

    SCORE

E   Feedback from the line manager on how the new
    recruit is settling in and performing   ✓
    It is worth finding out from managers how well new
    recruits are doing to assess how this compares with
    initial judgements.

    SCORE

F   Feedback from the new recruit   ✓
    It is important to check how the individual feels he/she
    is settling in and, as part of this process, you could ask
    for feedback on your role as an interviewer.

    SCORE

G   Feedback on the new recruit from others such as peers
    and customers   ✓
    This is a delicate area so proceed with caution. You
    would need permission from managers and individuals
    to undertake this and would have to be very clear
    about your purpose.

    SCORE

H Feedback from the line manager on the handling of
the process   ✓
It would be wise to clarify your outcome and prepare
some structured questions to ask the manager.

SCORE

I Review the selection process overall   ✓
You should ask yourself: 'What went well and what not
so well; how might the process be improved?'

SCORE

J Monitor the process for gender, ethnic group and/or
disability discrimination   ✓
This is something that, ideally, should be started as part
of the initial recruitment process and then monitored
up to selection point rather than subsequently.

SCORE

K Review the cost of the process against other selection
efforts   ✗
This would not serve any purpose as costs are likely to
vary. Also, is this within your province?

SCORE

L Compare the length of the process against other
selection exercises   ✗
Another task that wouldn't serve any real purpose.

SCORE

M Assess the cost of the process against its perceived
benefits   ✓
This is an essential task for anyone who is responsible
for the recruitment and selection process.

SCORE

Now add up your scores

TOTAL ASSESSMENT 10 SCORE

For assessment 10, the higher you score the better your grasp of what should be reviewed to evaluate the interview process.
The **maximum** score is **65**.
The **minimum** score is **0**.

So, how fit are you at follow-up? Look back to p.43 for your score for assessment 8 and write it down here ☐
Now your score for assessment 9 ☐
Now your score for assessment 10 ☐

Add these individual scores together to make your **total follow-up score:**

TOTAL FOLLOW-UP SCORE

The higher your total score, the better your ability to follow up interviews effectively.
The **maximum** score is **94**.
The **minimum** score is **4**.

 Well done, you are fit at follow-up. There is always room for improvement, however!

 You are reasonably fit at follow-up. However, there are some weaknesses so a work-out is in order!

 You have some understanding of effective follow-up, but that is not enough. You need to work-out to ensure you cover the gaps.

Your approach to following up after interviews is weak. You need to work-out to get fit in this area.

Ideally, you should now have worked through all 10 assessments and profiles. If so, read the page opposite to discover your **overall interviewing fitness level**.

If, however, you have chosen to focus on your follow-up skills ➡ Follow-up work-out p.83. Before doing this, though, it is wise to do some quick mental preparation ➡ Warm-up p.53.

How fit are your interviewing skills?

Ideally, you should now have completed all 10 assessments and profiles, and have a good idea of how fit you are in interviewing.

Personal fitness profile

Look back at how you scored in the three sections:
Preparation
Interviewing, and
Follow-up.

Make a note of your individual total scores for these sections below:

Preparation ☐
Interviewing ☐
Follow-up ☐

What is your total interviewing skills score?

TOTAL INTERVIEWING SKILLS SCORE

 Congratulations, you have a healthy level of skills. There is always room for improvement, however.
226-319

 You are moderately fit. You could do with building your fitness.
130-225

 You are not skills fit! You need to do some work on building your interviewing skills.
34-129

Now take another look at your individual total scores for the three sections. Circle these scores overleaf.

	UNFIT	REASONABLY FIT	FIT
Preparation	12-22	23-33	34-44
Interviewing	18-72	73-127	128-181
Follow-up	4-34	35-65	66-94

Are you strong or weak in any particular section/skills area? Are you, for example, strong at preparation but weak at follow-up? Or perhaps you have strengths and weaknesses across all sections? Look back to your individual scores in profiles 1-10. Can you identify any particular strengths or weaknesses?

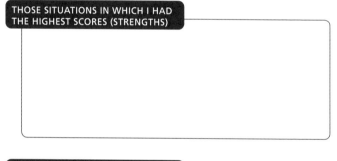

THOSE SITUATIONS IN WHICH I HAD THE HIGHEST SCORES (STRENGTHS)

THOSE SITUATIONS IN WHICH I HAD THE LOWEST SCORES (WEAKNESSES)

Congratulations on your strengths, but you do need to take action to develop your weaker areas.

Before moving on to Work-out, however, you need to do some quick mental preparation ➡ Warm-up p.53.

Warm-up

It is wise to do a quick mental warm-up before tackling the exercises in Work-out.

Take a few moments to reflect on why you want to improve your interviewing skills. Now imagine what it might be like to be more effective at interviewing. Think of yourself in a particular situation where you want to interview well...

How well prepared are you? ....
....

What do you look like?
My eye contact is ....
My body posture is ....

How well are you using your skills? ....
....

Are you building a rapport? ....

How is the candidate reacting?
The candidate is saying..
The candidate is being ....

How are you feeling?
I am feeling..

You are now ready to make this a reality.

If you have completed all 10 assessments ➡ Work-out p.55.
If, however, you have chosen to focus on a particular skills area/section
➡ Preparation work-out p.59.
➡ Interviewing work-out p.69.
➡ Follow-up work-out p.83.

Work-out

So, you've had your Fitness Assessment and identified your strengths and areas on which you need to work. Now is the time to take action!

Packed with practical exercises and activities, Work-out contains all the equipment you need to become super-fit at interviewing.

Look back at your personal fitness profile on p.51. Where do your strengths and weaknesses lie? Do they lie in specific areas of the skill – are you, for example, generally strong when it comes to preparing for an interview, but weak when it comes to follow-up? Or do they relate to all three skills areas? Depending on your personal fitness profile, you can either focus on improving a particular area of skill or work on individual weaknesses within each area.

Of course, if you do want to raise your level of performance in all areas then complete all the activities, then you really will be super-fit!

Work-outs 1-3 relate directly to profiles 1-3. Similarly, work-outs 4-7 and 8-10.

Preparation

Good preparation is key to success in selection interviewing. The following three work-outs will help you improve your preparation.

WORK-OUT 1: YOUR APPROACH

'I had six honest serving men, they taught me all I knew. Their names are "What" and "Why" and "When" and "How" and "Where" and "Who".'

Rudyard Kipling's quote is a great way of focusing the mind on what is needed at the start of any task, whether attending a meeting or running an interview.

For this exercise, you will need a sheet of plain paper.

1 Take your sheet of paper and write your task at the top. Then draw three columns down the page.

2 On the left-hand side make a note of the key words as illustrated by Kipling (starting with 'Who').

3 Using each word as a prompt, identify the key questions you need to ask. Make a note of these in the middle column.

4 Finally, on the right-hand side, answer each of the questions.

The following is an example prepared by a trainer.

Example

Task: Communication skills workshop		
Who	Who will I be doing it for?	The help desk team (6).
	Who else is involved?	Phil Brown (co-facilitator).
What	What is the purpose of the workshop?	To improve the team's telephone communication.
	What areas will I be covering?	General communication, using the telephone, body language.
	What outcome am I looking for?	By the end of training, team will be able to demonstrate more effective skills.
	What resources do I have available?	Training room, video, multi-media, flipcharts.
Why	Why is it being done?	The level of customer complaints has risen.
	Why am I doing it?	Specialist in communication training.
When	When will I be doing it?	Two-day course – 12 and 13 May, follow-up mid-June.
	When has it to be completed by?	End June.
How	How does it fit with other training?	Part of improving communications strategy for all staff.
	How will I be delivering it?	Group work and exercises, tutor feedback.
Where	Where will I be doing it?	In-house – training room.

Carry out this exercise each time you undertake a task. It should help you become more structured in your approach.

WORK-OUT 2: GATHERING INFORMATION

It is important that you are clear about what documentation is used in selection interviewing.

Checking out documentation
Obtain a copy of each of the following items and familiarize yourself with them.

For each form being used, make some key points for your own reference.

Document	Used in your selection process? ✓/ ✗	Example? (yes/no)	Key points
Job description			
Person specification			
Competency framework			
Exit interview			
Application form			
Assessment form			
Ethnic monitoring form			
Curriculum vitae			

Checking out requirements
Before you set up any interviews, review the job and the person needed for that job.

Use the following checklists.

Job checklist
If someone is leaving, check the job description:
✓ Has technology, new products or services changed the role?
✓ Has an exit interview been conducted that might highlight anything useful?
✓ Could key tasks be reallocated to others?

If it is a new job:
✓ Should it be full-time or part-time, fixed-term contract, flexible working?
✓ Should it be off-site working, term-time?
✓ Could it be a 'job-share'?
✓ Could it be contracted out?

If there isn't a job description, complete a job analysis:

> *Job descriptions should be clear, concise and unambiguous.*

✓ Gather relevant documentation (eg training manuals, organization charts, 'old' job descriptions etc).
✓ Identify the purpose, scope, key tasks and critical aspects of the role.
✓ Check out with the job holder, manager.
✓ Observe job being carried out over a period of time.
✓ Produce a draft job description.
✓ Check job description with key personnel.
✓ Amend, if necessary.

TRAINER'S TIP

Ideally a specialist (eg someone from HR/Personnel) should do a job analysis but use the expertise and knowledge of those closest to the job.

Person checklist
Check out the person specification
✓ Does it need amending?
✓ Do you need to review the criteria?

✓ Is a person specification framework available?

✓ If not, do you need to develop a framework?

✓ Have you identified essential and desirable criteria?

✓ Do the criteria need weighting?

> *Use these general classifications:*
> * *qualifications*
> * *experience*
> * *abilities*
> * *knowledge*
> * *circumstances*
> * *personality.*

Designing forms

If you identify a form which you think is necessary then complete this exercise.

Identify your reason for introducing the form. Then:

✓ Obtain examples from a range of sources.

✓ Identify the outcome you are looking for.

✓ Select the features that best meet your needs.

✓ Draft your own form.

✓ Get the views of a representative sample of colleagues on the design.

✓ Amend, if necessary.

✓ Pilot and re-adapt, if necessary.

✓ Implement the form.

> **TRAINER'S TIP**
>
> *The person specification should outline your 'ideal' candidate for the job. So, don't look for a computer scientist if all you want is basic keyboarding.*

WORK-OUT 3: ORGANIZING INTERVIEWS

Scheduling interviews

For each interview, you need to assess how much time is needed for:

1 Checking through the application and background documents beforehand.

2 The discussion with each candidate.

> **TRAINER'S TIP**
>
> *Use assessment forms if there is more than one interviewer. This will help with getting consistent feedback.*

3 Writing up notes.

4 Discussion with co-interviewers, where appropriate.

To help assess how much time you will need for interviews, first identify two different jobs in your organization. Select examples from different levels, such as middle manager and general assistant. Now, for each one, ask an experienced interviewer how many candidates they might reasonably schedule into a day. Make a note below.

Interviews can be one-to-one, two-to-one and panel. An assessment centre combines interviews with group exercises, tests and presentations.

	Maximum number of interviews in a day
Job 1:	
Job 2:	

Use this as a memory jogger when you do your own scheduling. Remember, don't try to cram in too much. If you have a number of candidates to see, be sensible about your capabilities and think about the need for fairness.

Preparing the environment
The physical environment in which you conduct interviews will affect both how a candidate, and interviewer, performs.

Discuss any proposed interview environment with an experienced interviewer. Using the chart opposite, draw up a list of key environmental aspects, making a note of why each aspect is important. (One has been done as an example.)

Key points about preparing the interview environment	
Key point	*Why it is important*
Brief reception staff	So they know who to expect when, and where to direct them.

How does your list of key points compare with the following?

Key points about preparing the interview environment	
Key point	*Why it is important*
Brief reception staff	To let them know who to expect and where they have to be directed.
Allocate a waiting area, preferably with some reading matter available (newspapers, brochures or PR materials)	Candidates should have somewhere to sit, and something to read
Check room booking	The 'best laid plans of mice and men' can go wrong. Leave nothing to chance.
Prepare a 'Do not disturb' sign	To ensure that no one tries to access the room.
Check with switchboard, if appropriate	To ensure all calls are redirected.

Check room for access	There may be candidates using wheelchairs.
Prepare layout	Set it up to get the best from the candidates.
Check temperature	To ensure the room is not too stuffy or too cold.
Check furniture	Ensure it is adequate and appropriate for the purpose.
Check cleanliness	Ensure it is tidy – a messy room gives a bad impression.
Check potential distractions (eg creaking furniture, traffic noise, harsh lights, bleeping computers)	To minimize interference with the discussion.

Dotting the i's and crossing the t's

As you get closer to the interviews, there are a number of final preparations you need to think about:

1 How will you structure the interview?
   This will vary according to the job and the situation but it is always useful to have a basic framework. This will help you to:
✓ Systematically collect data.
✓ Be fair to the candidates.
✓ Control the interview.
✓ Achieve the required outcome.

2 What documentation do you need to read?
✓ Job description and the person specification.
✓ Application forms/CVs/letters.
✓ The advertisement, if appropriate.
✓ If it is a second interview – previous interview notes.

3 What questions will you ask candidates?
✓ Plan questioning to assess competence, knowledge and personality.
✓ Compare the candidate information with the job description and the person specification (the 'ideal person').
✓ Make a note of candidates' experiences which are particularly relevant to the job to probe further.
✓ Check the relevant legislation.

Draw up a checklist for yourself to make sure you have covered everything.

Example

Checklist: Final touches	Yes	No	Comment
✓ Have I: • informed reception?			
• ensured the room is tidy?			
• checked access (wheelchairs, dogs)?			
• checked if communication/ language support needed (interpreter, loop system, translator)?			
✓ Do I know what the next stage of the selection process is?			
✓ Have I decided on a framework/structure for the interview?			
✓ Am I interviewing with others? If so, have we identified our roles?			

✓ Do I have:			
• job description/person spec?			
• application form/CV?			
• prepared questions?			
• background information on organization for candidates?			
• any other specific data?			
✓ Am I up to date with current legislation?			

Preparation checklist

✓ Who will you be interviewing? Check out the data on each candidate's application form, CV, application letter (if appropriate) and previous interview data (if appropriate).

✓ What do you want to achieve? Clarify the outcome; identify the aim of the process.

✓ What job is it? Check out what it looks like (job description) and what sort of person is needed (person specification). What background information is available?

✓ Why are you doing it? Why is the interview necessary (vacancy or new job)? Why have you been selected to interview?

✓ What stage is it? Check whether this is the first, second or final interview.

✓ How will you be doing it? Check the format of the interviews – one-to-one, two interviewers, a panel of interviewers? Check whether there will be tests.

✓ Where will you be doing it? Book the room, ensuring its suitability. Do a final check on the day.

Interviewing

The following three work-outs will help you develop your interviewing skills.

WORK-OUT 4: USING QUESTIONING SKILLS

Questions are useful only if they are the right questions. You need to be able to ask questions that will be understood by a candidate and get the information you are seeking. In other words:

- Will they be capable of doing the job?
- Will they want the job?
- Will they fit in with the team and the organization?
- Can you afford them?

'Closed' to 'open' questions

'Closed' questions usually get either a straightforward 'Yes' or 'No' response. You will also need to ask 'open' questions which encourage the candidate to give more information.

Read through the list of closed questions below and turn them into open questions. (The first has been done as an example.)

Closed question	Alternative open question
Does your manager get the best out of you?	How do you think your manager gets the best out of you?
Did you study Business?	
Do you get along with everyone?	
Did you find it easy to work as a team?	
Do you like detailed work?	
Do you get on with your colleagues?	
Do you have to make difficult decisions?	
Do you have any weaknesses?	
Can you work under pressure?	

Continue to practise this. You can, of course, also practise turning open questions into closed ones.

Question types

The question types we explored in assessment 4 were – open, open 'probing', closed, closed cliché, discriminatory, reflective, critical/assumptive, hypothetical, leading and multiple.

Look at the examples below.

Type of question	Example
open	'What are the advantages of a flatter structure organization?'
open 'probing'	'You said you enjoy team working. What is it that makes team working enjoyable?'
	'That sounds interesting, tell me more.' (encouraging); *'What happened next?'* (extension); *'So what were your specific responsibilities in the team?'* (clarifying)
closed	'I understand from what you've been saying that you would like to change direction in your career. Is that correct?'
closed cliché	'Do you like making difficult decisions?'
discriminatory	'What childcare arrangements will you have to make?'
reflective	'You seem to be irritated by the decision. So did you feel annoyed at the way the project was organized?'
critical/assumptive	'Your progress up the ladder hasn't been good – has it?'
hypothetical	'What would you do if your manager asked you to work late and you had a personal appointment?'
leading	'Isn't it right that we should have a no smoking policy?'
multiple	'What do you think caused the problem, what solutions did you consider and what was the outcome?'

You should be able to give examples of some of these from your own experience – either interviews you have had or meetings you have been involved in. Make a note of these below.

Type of question	Example
open	
open 'probing'	
closed	
closed cliché	
discriminatory	
reflective	
critical/ assumptive	
hypothetical	
leading	
multiple	

Continue to identify different question types – you don't need to be interviewing! You may be surprised at how quickly you begin to recognize them. Now all you need to do is use them appropriately.

Bear in mind the following tips:
✓ Follow a logical sequence with questions.
✓ Link questions to what candidates say: (*Candidate*) 'I received the quality award three times that year.' (*You*) 'You seem to have had a number of successes. What was your main achievement?'
✓ Ask open questions after closed ones. (*You*) 'How many staff report to you?' (*Candidate*) 'Five direct reports and one dotted line.' (*You*) 'What do you think are the key skills you need to manage your team?'

Reflection

This exercise will help you to reflect on whether or not you have used questions appropriately – and achieved a benefit.

Draw up a review sheet. You can use this as a general review, for example after meetings, when you have conducted interviews, following more casual discussions and so on.

1 Divide the review sheet into four columns. For example:

The question	Type	Used for?	Appropriate?

2 Make a note of the question on the left-hand side.

3 Identify the question type and its use in the middle columns.

4 Make a note of whether the question was appropriate or not – did it achieve any benefit?

5 Next identify any action you need to take by asking yourself:

A Could I have asked more appropriate questions? If so, what?

B Could my questioning have been more sensitive? If so, how?

C Were my questions in a logical sequence? If not, why not, and what would I do differently next time?

D If I had done things differently, would I have been clearer about the candidate's ability to do the job?

TRAINER'S WARNING

Don't avoid the negative – if you use questions inappropriately make a note and learn from your mistakes.

This is an extract from an interview review sheet.

The question	Type	Used for?	Appropriate?
'Did you have any difficulties getting here?'	Closed	Help candidate at beginning of interview to settle down	Yes
'You said you enjoyed your time in that department. Why do you think that was?'	Probing	To get further information	Yes
'The policies are bureaucratic, are they not?'	Leading	Getting candidate to agree with me!	No

WORK-OUT 5: USING EFFECTIVE LISTENING SKILLS

A good interviewer should be listening for about 70-75% of the time.

'Active' listening action sheet

Think about what you could do to make sure you listen actively during interviews. Use the five key areas below as headings:

TRAINER'S TIP

Allow silence – it gives candidates time to think!

1 Give full attention
2 Acknowledge
3 Reflect data
4 Reflect feelings
5 Summarize.

Now draw up a chart outlining the action you will take in each active listening area.

Example

Active listening | Action
Give full attention | Focus on the candidate.
Concentrate fully on what is being said, not on what I want to say next.
Don't let my mind wander!

Listening practice

You will need two colleagues (preferably experienced interviewers) to help with this exercise.

1   Copy the checklists that follow, or prepare your own.

2   Nominate one of your colleagues to speak ('Speaker') and one to observe ('Observer'). Give each colleague the appropriate checklist.

3   Ask the 'Speaker' to speak to you on a subject of their choice for approximately three minutes. Ask the 'Observer' to observe during the talk. (You should listen but ask any clarifying questions where necessary.)

TRAINER'S TIP

When changing to a new topic, summarize before you move on.

4   At the end of the time, you should summarize the talk.

5   Ask both colleagues to complete the assessments. (Get verbal feedback if this is appropriate.)

6   Finally, make notes on any improvements you could make to your listening.

Active listening: 'Speaker' assessment sheet			
KEY: 1 Usually 2 Sometimes 3 Never	1	2	3
Looked at me when I spoke?			
Reflected back what I said?			
Reflected back how I felt?			
Seemed relaxed, open and interested?			
Summarized what I said?			
Used encouraging body language (nodding, open body stance, leaning forward). Used verbal encouragement such as 'em', 'aha'?			
Interrupted only to ask relevant questions?			
Changed the subject?			
Fidgeted or distracted me?			
Used negative body language ('closed' body stance, negative expressions and gestures)?			
Agreed with points rather than argued against them?			
Made me feel that I was being listened to?			

Active listening: 'Observer' assessment sheet			
KEY: 1 Usually 2 Sometimes 3 Never	1	2	3
Looked at the Speaker during the exercise?			
Reflected back what the Speaker said?			
Reflected back how the Speaker felt?			
Seemed relaxed, open and interested?			
Summarized what the Speaker said?			
Used encouraging body language (nodding, open body stance, leaning forward). Used verbal encouragement such as 'mm', 'aha'?			
Interrupted only to ask relevant questions?			

Changed the subject?			
Fidgeted or distracted the Speaker?			
Used negative body language (closed body stance, negative expressions and gestures)?			
Agreed with points rather than argued against them?			
Seemed to make the Speaker feel they were being listened to?			

WORK-OUT 6: BODY LANGUAGE

Communication signals (body language) are the non-verbal messages we send one another. They cover how close we stand to someone, our stance and posture, making eye contact, our facial expression, how we move our heads, the gestures we make, how we use our voice and 'non-verbal' noises such as 'em' and 'oh'.

In an interview, there are two aspects to body language – your own and the candidate's.

To give a professional image as an interviewer you need to use positive body language, avoiding any negative signals. Some key points:

✓ Keep your distance. (Research suggests 90-130cm apart is appropriate.)
✓ Sit up straight.
✓ Use a firm handshake.
✓ Walk tall.
✓ Lean slightly forward and keep your body directed towards the candidate.
✓ Maintain eye contact – too little and the candidate may feel cut off, too much and the candidate may feel intimidated.
✓ Avoid negative facial expressions – showing irritation, boredom, disbelief or sarcasm.

✓ Use head movements appropriately – nodding and shaking.
✓ Use gestures that convey calmness – open, smooth and easy.
✓ Avoid fiddling, sniffing, tapping or pointing fingers, tapping feet, doodling.

Improving your communication signals
For this exercise, sit down in front of a mirror and visualize yourself in an interview situation. Use a 'real' example if you can – either an interview you have conducted or one you are about to do. Work through the interview, observing your body language throughout. Make notes on areas that need improving.

Try and become more aware of your communication signals. For example, if you are in a meeting, in the office or out with friends, make mental notes of how effective you are at reinforcing your message through your body language. Use the list below to reflect on your use of signals and help you to improve.

Communication signal	Used? ✓/✗	Appropriate? ✓/✗	If yes, why? If no, why not?
Facial expressions • smiling • frowning • raising eyebrows • grinning • glaring			
Stance/posture • sitting straight • walking tall • leaning forward • leaning back • rocking			

Handshake – solid			
Eye contact • none • frequent • staring			
Arms • open and relaxed • folded			
Proximity • too close • acceptable • far away			
Finger gestures • pointing • shaking • tapping			
Hand gestures • by sides • open • closed • clenched • on hips • moving quickly • fisted			
Head movements • nodding • shaking			
Non-verbal 'noises' eg 'mm', 'aha', 'oh', 'heh'			
Personal mannerisms • fiddling with items • doodling • sniffing • any others?			

People watch

1 Next time you are in a meeting, study the body language of your colleagues. What do they do to emphasize, get attention, interject, put over arguments and so on? Watch out for any signs of distress – what are they? Make notes on key points.

TRAINER'S WARNING

Remember, people from different cultural backgrounds may use and interpret body language differently.

2 Turn the sound down on the TV and try interpreting what is going on from the body language. Even better, if you have a video, record the programme. Then play it back with sound once you have watched it. How accurate were you in your observations?

3 Observe people meeting for the first time. What body language do they use? What is their proximity? Note down the key points.

4 When you are in a restaurant or at a party, study those around you. Using their body language as clues, identify those who might:
   • be having a friendly discussion
   • be romantically linked
   • have little to say to each other
   • be arguing
   • be strangers.

TRAINER'S TIP

Close friends or colleagues in deep discussion will often mirror each other's body language, eg positioning their arms/ legs/ body similarly.

WORK-OUT 7: BUILDING A RAPPORT

It is your job to make the interview run smoothly and to make it as positive an experience as possible. You want candidates to be calm and respond honestly; you don't want them to get a negative impression of either you or your organization. It is essential that you build rapport from the start.

If you use your questioning, listening and communication signals effectively, you will help to build a rapport with candidates. But there are other things you can do to build rapport!

Setting the scene
Think about an interview you attended which made you feel positive from the outset. What was it that made the first minutes so effective? Make notes.

For example, your list could include:
• a friendly, welcoming greeting
• an explanation of the purpose
• details of the structure and timing given.

You can also establish rapport quickly by chatting briefly to relax the candidate. Draw up a list of general questions that you might find useful, for example, 'Did you have a good journey?'; 'Did you get caught in the thunder storm?' Obviously, as you become more experienced, you can abandon the list as putting candidates at ease should come naturally.

TRAINER'S TIP

Don't go on too long – candidates will want to get to the 'nitty gritty' of the interview.

TRAINER'S WARNING

Research has shown that interviewers often make their minds up within the first four minutes and then spend the rest of the interview looking for information to *back up their decision.*

Bringing down barriers

Watch out for concious or unconcious 'barriers' to fair selection. Be aware of your attitudes and behaviours – and how they affect your judgement.

Look through the barriers below. Tick those you feel might be a problem for you; reflect on why they are a challenge to you. Now draw up your own list and keep it in a prominent place to remind you of your barriers!

Barrier	Explanation/examples	✓
Making instant judgements	'Scruffy – probably lazy' 'Well-spoken and positive – must be very intelligent' 'Never did like red hair!'	
The 'halo' effect	Thinking a candidate who scores highly against one or two of the criteria is 'perfect'	
The 'horns' effect	Believing a candidate who is unable to produce evidence to meet a criterion must be unsuitable	
Contrast	Rating an average candidate lower who comes after an outstanding one and vice versa	
Similarity	Liking those who are similar to ourselves and rating them more highly than those who are different from us	
First impressions	Looking for information to back up an initial positive or negative assessment	
Lack of empathy	Taking an instant dislike to someone – making it difficult to be objective	

Taking notes

Unless you have a photographic memory, you will need to take notes. They jog your memory on points that need probing later and they are also essential for the final assessment of candidates. The downside is that note-taking can interfere with maintaining rapport.

Use these guidelines to help you write effective notes, while maintaining rapport:

✓ First, always inform the candidate that you will be taking notes.

✓ Divide your page into a positive and negative side and enter notes appropriately. Use symbols where possible, eg an eye for eye contact, a line for a smile and so on.

✓ Jot down key words or facts only but ensure you record anything that needs subsequent action.

✓ Keep your head up as much as possible; maintain eye contact with candidates.

✓ Write legibly and accurately.

✓ Don't allow your notes to become more important than the candidate.

✓ Sit so that the candidate cannot see what you are writing.

✓ Make a point of writing when candidates are highlighting information they think is important.

✓ Beware of making derogatory points – they might be challenged later!

If your note-taking is not up to it, think about recording the interview. However, you will need to get permission from the candidate, and make sure that batteries are full and the machine works OK.

Interviewing checklist

✓ Use open and closed questions appropriately.
✓ Follow a logical sequence with your questioning.
✓ Use active listening skills – pay attention, acknowledge, reflect data and feelings, and summarize.
✓ Practise and use positive communication signals.
✓ Practise reading communication signals.
✓ Check that candidates' communication signals are in congruence with what they are saying.
✓ Build and maintain a rapport with candidates:
  • use effective interviewing skills
  • watch out for potential barriers
  • take notes effectively but unobtrusively.

Follow-up

WORK-OUT 8: EVALUATING

Making your decision on the 'best' candidate is crucial. If you don't make as informed a choice as possible then all your good work in preparing and interviewing could be wasted – and costly.

TRAINER'S TIP

Even the best candidate won't be 'perfect'. If you highlight any potential shortcomings at interview, these can be addressed as part of the initial training.

You will need to produce a report based on any notes you have made. Evaluation statements must be clear. For example: *'The candidate was experienced in teamworking – for two years she has been part of a small project team'* rather than *'The candidate has good teamwork'*.

If you have interviewed with others and have differences in opinion, discuss your perceptions and notes. If there are wide variances these should be examined closely.

TRAINER'S WARNING

Test results should form part of any evaluation.

Don't be tempted to select a candidate just for the sake of it. If your decision is difficult, you may need to think about setting tests, starting the process again or re-evaluating your criteria. Further costs now may save much greater costs in the future!

TRAINER'S WARNING

Candidates should be reviewed against the job and person criteria, not against each other.

Advice and practice

1   Discuss the evaluation process with experienced interviewers. Find out what action they take. Make notes on the key points.

2   Draw up a suitable assessment sheet to use when you interview each candidate. (You may need more than one!) Discuss your draft with your experienced colleagues and amend it, if necessary.

Below is an extract from an assessment sheet for a hotel receptionist.

Example

	Assessment	Comment
KEY: 1 = Poor match to criteria **2** = More weaknesses than strengths **3** = More strengths than weaknesses **4** = Good match		
	1 2 3 4	
Appearance		
Is the candidate acceptable?	1 2 3 4	
Voice – good quality and speech clear	1 2 3 4	
Clothes – smart and neat	1 2 3 4	
Manner – easy and confident	1 2 3 4	
Attainments		
Has candidate sufficient knowledge/skills?	1 2 3 4	
GCSE including English	1 2 3 4	
Computer skills (Word and Excel)	1 2 3 4	
Experience in hotels or similar receptionist role	1 2 3 4	

3   Arrange to observe some interviews (either real or role
    plays) and complete assessments for these. Review your
    evaluations with the interviewers. Discuss differences
    and make notes on the key points.

WORK-OUT 9: INFORMING CANDIDATES

Keeping candidates waiting can be distressing, is
unprofessional and does nothing for the image of the
organization. So, even if some candidates have been short-
listed for a second interview, anyone who doesn't meet the
job requirements can be eliminated immediately.

Make a note of the reasons for not appointing unsuitable
candidates. This helps you to give feedback should they ask,
but more importantly, it could be crucial if there is a challenge
on any grounds, eg perceived discrimination.

Informing candidates

1   Make a note of the procedure for rejecting candidates
    in your organization. Is there anything that could be
    improved? If so, what? Make a proposal outlining your
    suggestions and pass it to the relevant individual.

    If there isn't a procedure, perhaps you should think
    about implementing one together with a standard.

    For example:
    • The principal interviewer will be responsible for
      informing those candidates they have interviewed.
    • All unsuccessful candidates will be informed by
      telephone/letter within one/two weeks of interview.

2 Develop an outline which you could use as the basis for a rejection letter. Make sure that you individualize it effectively for each unsuccessful candidate.

3 Think back to when you were last interviewed. Now think about what you might like to have heard as feedback. Use this to prepare a script for giving feedback. This should help you to give meaningful, specific feedback – without waffle!

WORK-OUT 10: REVIEWING THE PROCESS

Your continuing professional development is important; one way to contribute to this is to review your efforts and learn from them. There are three areas to consider:

1 Your skills and judgement.

2 The interviewing process (ie organizational efforts).

3 The quality of the successful candidate.

Draw up a list of the key areas to be reviewed. From this, produce an assessment sheet for yourself. You may want to make this a two-part document – one for completion as soon as possible after the interview process has been finalized, the other for completion at an interval (three-six months, depending on the project).

Example

Personal assessment sheet					
KEY: 1= Showed some significant weaknesses **2** = Showed some minor weaknesses **3** = Met requirements **4** = Above average **5** = Outstanding					
Project: To fill the post of Production Assistant for the PR department					
Part 1 (14.01.03)	1	2	3	4	5
How well did I prepare?	1	2	3	<u>4</u>	5
How effective were my interview skills? • Questioning	1	2	<u>3</u>	4	5
• Listening	1	2	3	<u>4</u>	5
• Behaving assertively (incorporating communication signals)	1	2	<u>3</u>	4	5
How did my co-interviewers rate my performance?	1	2	<u>3</u>	4	5
How clear was my evaluation?	1	2	3	<u>4</u>	5
How professionally did I handle the rejections?	1	2	3	<u>4</u>	5
How well did I give feedback?	1	2	3	<u>4</u>	5
How well did I feel I handled the project?	1	2	<u>3</u>	4	5
How well did the 'client' (the department/ manager for whom interviewing project undertaken) think I handled the project?	1	2	<u>3</u>	4	5
Part 2 (15.06.03)	1	2	3	4	5
How do I rate my evaluation now that the employee has been in post for six months?	1	2	3	<u>4</u>	5
How well has the new employee settled in?	1	2	3	<u>4</u>	5
How effective is he/she in the role – the employee's perspective	1	2	<u>3</u>	4	5
How effective is he/she in the role – the manager's perspective	1	2	3	<u>4</u>	5
As a result of the above assessment, I intend to: • practise my interviewing skills – volunteer for more projects • identify a suitable course where I will get role play practice • do some video practice with Jan?					

Follow-up checklist

✓ Evaluate all candidates – write reports and/or complete assessment sheets, preferably using previously identified criteria.

✓ Ensure candidates are evaluated against the criteria for the job, not each other.

✓ Don't select a candidate just to fill a vacancy; if necessary, start the process again.

✓ Inform unsuccessful candidates as soon as possible but, if appropriate, keep one or two reserves provided they are not kept waiting too long.

✓ Review the process:
  • from a personal 'How did I do?' point of view
  • its organization and effectiveness, and
  • the success of the project, ie 'Was he/she the "best" candidate for the job?'

Keeping Fit

Keeping Fit

Well, congratulations on finishing the book! Hopefully you have enjoyed the experience and gained from the advice and insights offered.

As you have discovered, interviewing is a powerful, and empowering, skill. But like any skill, practice makes perfect, and the more you interview, the better you will get at it. You need to keep skills fit, and this is what the final part of the book is all about...

Keeping fit

As mentioned at the very start of this book, interviewing is a key skill for success both at work and home, and it is important you don't let it slip.

You need to keep on your toes, keep practising. If you feel your skills slipping then look through the book again, remind yourself of the key learning points, even run through a couple of exercises. Better still, set yourself some real-life targets *now* to keep yourself up to scratch.

Make a note of your targets in your personal fitness plan below (bearing in mind the benefits it will bring you, or others). Specify actions and time-scales; this will keep you focused and fit.

Personal fitness plan

Action	By when	✓
......	......	......
......	......	......
......	......	......
......	......	......
......	......	......
......	......	......
......	......	......
......	......	......
......	......	......
......	......	......
......	......	......
......	......	......

Further Reading/Resources

Further reading/resources

There is a wealth of resources available if you want more information or advice about interviewing.

Books
Fowler, Alan, *Writing Job Descriptions*, CIPD, 2000
Furnham, Adrian, *Body Language at Work*, CIPD, 1999
Hindle, Tim, *Interviewing Skills*, Dorling Kindersley, 1998

Videos
Out of the Question, Capita Learning & Development